PAYING for COLLEGE

A 2015 Guide to
Saving Time and Money

Mark Bilotta

Please send all inquiries to:
CollegeValue®, LLC
PO Box 20113
Worcester MA 01602-0113
inquiry@collegevalue.info

ISBN-13: 978-1496180735
ISBN-10: 1496180739

Contents

Preface

If it weren't so long, I would have titled this book: *Paying for College: A 2015 Guide to Saving Time and Money Before, During and After College.* The reality for many students and families today is that saving and paying for college could extend over three or four *decades.*

I've been in higher education for more than 25 years, 14 of those years at the senior level. I've had the opportunity to work with both highly selective and less-selective private and public colleges and universities. And just as rewarding, I oversaw a statewide network of federally funded higher education access programs.

I've watched as students and families have struggled to understand the college search and selection process. And as college costs continued to soar, it became clear that students and families need to recognize early in the process that it's no longer just about finding the right *academic fit*, it has to be a good *financial fit* as well.

While this book has been written to help students and families make better-informed decisions, it's also meant to give the thousands of school counselors and other education advisors a better working knowledge about college as a good *financial fit*.

For those working with students and families, and to the many committed parents, I offer the following inspirational story as a reminder of why we do what we do. Know that your unwavering commitment to your children and students will impact lives for generations to come.

"Once upon a time, there was a wise man who used to go to the ocean to do his writing. He had a habit of walking on the beach before he began his work.

One day, as he was walking along the shore, he looked down the beach and saw a human figure moving like a dancer. He smiled to himself at the thought of someone who would dance to the day, and so, he walked faster to catch up.

As he got closer, he noticed that the figure was that of a young man, and that what he was doing was not dancing at all. The young man was reaching down to the shore, picking up small objects, and throwing them into the ocean.

He came closer still and called out "Good morning! May I ask what it is that you are doing?" The young man paused, looked up, and replied "Throwing starfish into the ocean."

"I must ask, then, why are you throwing starfish into the ocean?" asked the somewhat startled wise man.

To this, the young man replied, "The sun is up and the tide is going out. If I don't throw them in, they'll die."

Upon hearing this, the wise man commented, "But, young man, do you not realize that there are miles and miles of beach and there are starfish all along every mile? You can't possibly make a difference!"

At this, the young man bent down, picked up yet another starfish, and threw it into the ocean. As it met the water, he said, "It made a difference for that one."

— Loren Eiseley

Introduction

Students and families can't control a college's costs, but they CAN control their own college spending.

Much has been written about selecting a college for its *academic fit*, but not enough on selecting a college for its *financial fit*.

Financing a college education, whether it's a certificate, associate, bachelor or graduate degree program, isn't just about getting in. It's about staying and successfully completing a program on time. Or, as we say in higher education, it's about access, retention and completion.

The practical information contained in this book is designed to help students, families, school counselors, and others make more informed decisions about these college-related financial challenges and opportunities.

The chapters in this book appear in somewhat of a chronological order, starting with saving for college and moving through actions that can be taken as early as middle school. Each short chapter is written to explain just one concept, like *net price* or *preferential packaging*, or *reverse transfer*.

The chapters can be read in order, or perused for timely and needed information or clarification. They are intentionally short, designed as a quick read, and conclude with where to turn for additional resources and details.

Keep in mind as you read that price doesn't always dictate quality. I can tell you from experience that tuition prices are sometimes set based on an institution's competitors' prices. Some enrollment managers refer to this as the "Chivas Regal effect," implying that the public will perceive a higher-priced institution as better than a lower-priced one. Don't fall for it!

In the end, I hope readers will have a better working knowledge of college as a good *financial fit* and feel more confident in the college decisions made or advice provided.

1   Saving for College

> *Saving for college, regardless of the amount, sets the tone in the home that college is attainable.*

Saving for a college education can be a daunting task. Some families start early with newborns. Others may delay until elementary, middle or even high school. By some estimates, more than 70 percent of families actively save for a child's education.

However, some families may feel they'll never be able to save enough, so they don't even bother to start. To them, I offer the results of a 2013 report from The Assets and Education Initiative (AEDI) at the University of Kansas School of Social Welfare that found that

> *"...even having a few hundred dollars in savings designated for education is significantly associated with a child's educational outcomes: low- and moderate-income students with up to $500 designated for college are three times more likely to enroll and four times more likely to graduate from college than their peers with no savings for college."*

There are plenty of articles and even entire books that can provide greater details about long-term savings plans. The following is offered in the spirit of providing a general "working knowledge" of two of the larger plans.

5

Qualified Tuition Programs (QTPs) - 529 Plans

- A qualified tuition program is typically set up by a state or eligible educational institution, to allow a family to either prepay *(tuition prepayment plan)* or contribute to an account *(tuition savings account)* established for paying a student's qualified education expenses at an eligible educational institution.

- States are free to offer one or both plans.

- Student must be enrolled at least half-time.

- Qualified educational expenses include tuition and fees, books, supplies and equipment. Room and board expenses may also qualify.

Coverdell Education Savings Accounts (ESAs)

- Banks and other IRS-approved entities offer Coverdell ESAs.

- Contribution eligibility is tied to income: modified adjusted gross income must be less than $110,000 ($220,000 if filing a joint return).

- Maximum allowable contribution per beneficiary (student) is $2,000 per year.

- Amounts in the accounts grow tax free until distributed.

- Student must be enrolled at least half-time.

- Qualified educational expenses include tuition and fees, books, supplies and equipment. Room and board expenses may also qualify.

BTW

Many states have creative names for their plans, such as ScholarShare (CA), Path2College (GA) and U.Plan (MA). It's important to know the details before making a long-term financial commitment. If you really like details, check out the IRS Publication 970!

Additional Resources

- IRS Publication 970 – Tax Benefits for Education

- State listing of Qualified Tuition Plans (QTP) – www.collegesavings.org

2 Sticker Price vs. Net Price

Few college students pay the sticker price. What most students actually pay is the net price.

Sticker Price

Shopping for a college today sounds more like shopping for a car. A phrase often heard is *sticker price*. What is sticker price? In most cases, it refers to the advertised price.

For example, if you browse a college's website, you might find something like this:

Tuition and Fees $30,000
Room and Board $10,000

The figures typically represent the annual price for a full-time student. The room and board price may represent an average cost, based on housing accommodations and meal plan option.

Sticker Price = Cost of Attendance (COA)

The *cost of attendance* typically refers to the total cost a student will incur for a full academic year. *Cost of attendance* includes:

- Tuition and fees (see Glossary for definitions)
- Room and board (or a housing and food allowance)
- Books and supplies
- Transportation

9

- Other educational costs, such as a computer or special needs

Here's an example of the *cost of attendance* at a private, 4-year college.

Table 2: Cost of Attendance (full time for one year)	
Tuition and Fees	$30,000
Room and Board	$10,000
Books and Supplies	$1,200
Transportation	$1,000
Other educational or personal expenses	$1,900
TOTAL COST OF ATTENDANCE	$44,100

Net Price

Net price, on the other hand, is what a student will actually pay. It takes the *cost of attendance* and subtracts any grants and scholarships that a student receives. Remember, grants and scholarships are monies that don't need to be paid back.

Cost of Attendance
- Grants & Scholarships
= Net Price

Example

A student is accepted to College X, which has a *cost of attendance* of $48,550. The student is offered $23,525 in federal, state and institutional grants and scholarships. The *net price* (what a student will actually pay) is $25,025.

Cost of Attendance	$48,550
Grants & Scholarships	- $23,525
Net Price	= $25,025

10

Importance of Net Price

At first glance, a college's *sticker price* may be somewhat shocking. In 2013-2014, some institutions' *cost of attendance* was more than $60,000. However, a large number of students will qualify for grants and scholarships. In those cases, the *net price* (what a student will actually pay), may be much lower than the *sticker price* and much more affordable.

BTW

More detail about net price is presented in Chapter 6 when the discussion moves to the federally mandated *net price calculators* now required on every college and university website.

3 Expected Family Contribution (EFC)

It's important that students and families get an early estimate of their Expected Family Contribution (EFC), perhaps even as early as middle school.

How do the government and colleges determine what a family can pay towards a student's college expenses?

It is determined when a student files the *Free Application for Federal Student Aid*, more commonly known as the FAFSA. (*More on filing the FAFSA later.*) As a result of filing the *FAFSA*, a student receives a report with an index number used by colleges to determine how much federal student aid the student can receive and, to some extent, how much money the family is expected to contribute for one year's college expenses. This index number is the *Expected Family Contribution (EFC)*.

The reason *Expected Family Contribution (EFC)* is listed early in this book is to emphasize how important it is for students and families to get early estimates of their *Expected Family Contribution* - as early as 9th grade, perhaps even middle school.

Why is it important to know a family's EFC early on?

All too often, families may think that college is unaffordable. Such thinking may discourage a student and family from even considering college. If attending college isn't likely, why should a student be encouraged to take the most rigorous courses? Can you see the domino effect?

You wouldn't file a FAFSA in the 9th grade to get an estimate of a family's expected contribution. To accomplish that, there are some great *Expected Family Contribution (EFC)* calculators online that can provide it. One worth noting is offered by the College Board, found at www.bigfuture.collegeboard.org

As Table 3A shows, there are basically five steps to calculating a family's *Expected Family Contribution (EFC)*, based primarily on available income and assets.

EFC Calculator

Table 3A: Expected Family Contribution Calculator	
Step 1	Determine a student's status: Dependent or Independent
Step 2	Pick a Formula
	- Federal Methodology (FM)
	- Institutional Methodology (IM)
	- Both FM and IM
Step 3	Family Information
Step 4	Student Information
Step 5	Finances
	- Dependent Student and Parent Income OR Independent Student Income
	- Allowances
	- Assets
Results	EFC ($) using the Federal Methodology (FM)
	EFC ($) using the Institutional Methodology (IM)
	Source: College Board

Notice there are two different methodologies (or formulas) used to calculate the EFC. Two of the major differences are highlighted on the next page in Table 3B.

14

Table 3B: Key Differences Between Methodologies	
Federal Methodology (FM)	**Institutional Methodology (IM)**
Used to determine _federal aid_ eligibility	Used to determine _institutional aid_ eligibility
Does <u>not</u> consider home equity	Considers home equity and other resources

Example

The following table shows three examples of Expected Family Contribution (EFCs). These examples assume a family of four, with one student preparing to enter college for the first time. The figures are estimates only.

Table 3C: Examples of Expected Family Contribution (EFC)			
	Example 1	**Example 2**	**Example 3**
Parents' Adjusted Gross Income	$20,000	$60,000	$150,000
Student's Adjusted Gross Income	$4,000	$4,000	$4,000
Parents' Assets	$ 0	$ 0	$10,000
Student's Assets	$ 0	$ 0	$2,000
Home Equity	$ 0	$125,000	$125,000
Expected Family Contribution using the Federal Methodology	$ 0	$4,800	$32,000
Expected Family Contribution using the Institutional Methodology	$ 0	$8,000	$29,000
Note: These are only estimates.			

Automatic Zero EFC or Simplified Needs Test

Families with lower incomes should explore whether they qualify for one of the following two options:

- Automatic Zero EFC – If parent(s) have a combined adjusted gross income of $24,000 or less and are eligible to file their taxes using the 1040A or 1040 EZ form, the family's Expected Family Contribution (EFC) is $0.

- Simplified Needs Test (SNT) – If parent(s) have a combined adjusted gross income of $49,999 or less and are eligible to file their taxes using the 1040A or 1040EZ, then all assets are ignored using the federal methodology.

If a family has more than one child attending college at the same time, the federal formula divides the Expected Family Contribution (EFC) by the number of children in college. For example, if a family's EFC is $10,000, with two children in college, the EFC is divided in half, $5,000 per child. The institutional formula uses a slightly different breakdown.

Additional Resources

- Expected Family Contribution (EFC) – www.ifap.ed.gov/efcformulaguide/attachments/091913EFCFor mulaGuide1415.pdf

- Expected Family Contribution (EFC) Calculator – www.bigfuture.collegeboard.org

4   Financial Aid

> *More than 70 percent of all undergraduates*
> *receive some type of financial aid.*

The cost of college can appear very expensive if a student and family just see the *sticker price*. But when you consider the *net price* (what a student will actually pay), the price may look a little better.

However, for most families, even the *net price* looks too expensive. That's where *financial aid* comes into the picture. *Financial aid* helps meet a student's demonstrated *financial need*.

Most families will show *financial need*, which is defined as:

$$\begin{aligned} &\text{Cost of Attendance} \\ -\ &\underline{\text{Expected Family Contribution}} \\ =\ &\text{Financial Need} \end{aligned}$$

Example

If a college had a cost of attendance of $40,000, and the student and family had an Expected Family Contribution (EFC) of $5,000, their financial need would be $35,000.

Cost of Attendance	$40,000
Expected Family Contribution	- $ 5,000
Financial Need	= $35,000

Financial aid is available from a number of different sources:
- Federal Government
- State Government
- Colleges and universities
- Banks and other private lenders
- Private and nonprofit organizations

Here's a breakdown of the types of aid and who offers them:

Table 4: Types of Financial Aid	
TYPE	**DESCRIPTION**
GRANTS	
Federal Pell Grant	• Financial aid that doesn't have to be repaid • Students must show financial need • Maximum award: $5,645 per year • Available for up to 12 semesters
Federal Supplemental Educational Opportunity Grant (FSEOG)	• Financial aid that doesn't have to be repaid • Students must show significant financial need • Maximum award: $4,000 per year • Administered by a college's financial aid office • Deadlines vary by college
State Grants	• Financial aid that doesn't have to be repaid • Amounts and deadlines vary by state
SCHOLARSHIPS	
State	• Financial aid that doesn't have to be repaid • Awards based on financial need and/or merit • Amounts and deadlines vary by state
College	• Financial aid that doesn't have to be repaid • Usually does not require a separate application • Amounts and deadlines vary by college

Table 4: Types of Financial Aid	
TYPE	**DESCRIPTION**
Private	<ul><li>Financial aid that doesn't have to be repaid</li><li>Amounts and deadlines vary</li></ul>
LOANS	
Federal Direct Subsidized Stafford Loan	<ul><li>Must be repaid with interest</li><li>Based on financial need</li><li>Maximum amount: $3,500-$5,500 per year</li><li>Interest is paid by government while in school (*subsidized*)</li><li>Student is the borrower</li></ul>
Federal Direct Unsubsidized Stafford Loan	<ul><li>Must be repaid with interest</li><li>No requirement to demonstrate financial need</li><li>College determines maximum amount</li><li>Interest accrues while in college (unsubsidized)</li><li>Student is the borrower</li></ul>
Federal Perkins Loan	<ul><li>Must be repaid with interest</li><li>Students must show significant financial need</li><li>Maximum award: $5,500 per year</li><li>Administered by a college's financial aid office</li><li>Deadlines vary by college</li><li>Student is the borrower</li></ul>
Direct PLUS Loan	<ul><li>Must be repaid with interest</li><li>Maximum amounts vary</li><li>Requires a credit check</li><li>U.S. Dept. of Education is the lender</li><li>Parent is the borrower</li></ul>

Table 4: Types of Financial Aid	
TYPE	**DESCRIPTION**
Private	• Must be repaid with interest • Maximum amount varies • Issued by a lender such as a bank or credit union • Parent or student is the borrower
WORK-STUDY	
Federal Work-Study	• Based on financial need • Provides part-time employment while in college (*most students will use as spending money*) • Administered by participating colleges
TAX CREDITS	
American Opportunity Credit	• Maximum tax credit: up to $2,500 per student • Must be income eligible • Can be claimed for only four tax years
Lifetime Learning Credit	• Maximum tax credit: up to $2,000 per tax return • Must be income eligible • No limit on number of years to claim credit
TAX DEDUCTIONS	
Student Loan Interest Deduction	• Maximum deduction: $2,500 • Based on income
Tuition and Fee Deduction	• Maximum deduction: $4,000 • Based on income

Work-study money is paid directly to the student at least once a month, based on the number of hours worked. Most jobs are on campus, although the federal government requires a minimum of 7% of a college's work-study allocation be used to employ students in community service jobs. Many students will use this money for discretionary spending. It's worth noting that some students will strategize to get a work-study job that relates to their intended field of study.

Additional Resources

- Federal Financial Aid – www.studentaid.ed.gov

- IRS Publication 970 – Tax Benefits for Education

5   *FAFSA4caster*

The federal government's online tools are a great way of getting early estimates for federal financial aid.

*F*AFSA4caster provides an estimate of federal financial aid for one academic year. It's based on the information entered and certain assumptions such as full-time attendance. Estimates include:

- Federal Pell Grant
- Federal Work-Study (based on the average nationally)
- Federal Direct Stafford Loans

In the following table, we continue to use our example of a family of four, with one student preparing to enter college for the first time.

Table 5: *FAFSA4caster*	Example 1	Example 2	Example 3
Parents' Adjusted Gross Income (AGI)	$20,000	$60,000	$150,000
Student's Adjusted Gross Income (AGI)	$4,000	$4,000	$4,000
Federal Pell Grant *(estimate)*	$5,645	$1,595	$ 0
Federal Work-Study	$1,465	$1,465	$1,465
Direct Stafford Loan	$5,500	$5,500	$5,500

Additional Resources
- *FAFSA4caster* –
  http://studentaid.ed.gov/fafsa/estimate

23

6   Net Price Calculator

There's no need to wait until April of senior year to get an estimate of your financial aid award.

U p to now, students and families have had to guess what their financial aid award might be if a student was accepted to a specific college. However, for the past few years, the federal government has mandated that colleges and universities provide *net price calculators* on their websites. Remember, *net price* is what a student will actually pay. These online tools are designed to give a specific student an estimate of what that student might receive in financial aid from that specific college. Here's how it works.

Some *net price* calculators are more helpful than others. Typically, the more information requested, the better the estimate. Information requested may include:

- Household information such as number of family members, age of older parent, etc.

- Parent(s) and student incomes and asset information

- SAT or ACT scores

- High school Grade Point Average (GPA)

To give you an example of just how helpful these net price calculators can be, Table 6 was created based on:

- Family of four
- Parents' adjusted gross income: $60,000
- Student's adjusted gross income: $4,000
- Student's GPA: 3.9
- Student's SAT (Critical Reading and Math scores): 1400

The schools used in Table 6 represent small and large *endowments*. *Endowments* are a school's financial investments that pay interest. A percentage of that interest each year is used to support the college's priorities. In many cases, those priorities include scholarships. Some scholarships may be need-based; others may be merit-based.

A school with a large *endowment* (there are more than 70 with endowments greater than $1 billion) can offer much more institutional scholarship aid than an institution with less than $20 million.

Note that the lower-priced, 4-year public and the highest priced, 4-year private with a large *endowment* have almost the same *net price* (what a student will actually pay.) College C, with the large *endowment*, offered an Institutional Grant (need-based) of $45,150. College B, with the smaller *endowment*, could only offer a $15,000 Institutional Scholarship (merit-based.) This is one reason why students and families should not dismiss a school from consideration just because of a high *sticker price* and why knowing a college's *endowment* may help in a student's search for a good *financial fit*.

	College A 4-Year Public; Small Endowment	College B 4-Year Private; Small Endowment	College C 4-Year Private; Large Endowment
Table 6: NET PRICE CALCULATORS			
Estimated Cost of Attendance (COA)			
Tuition and Fees	$8,080	$32,760	$46,088
Room and Board	$9,520	$11,960	$12,884
Books and Supplies	$2,000	$960	$1,000
Transportation	$750	$1,200	$ 0
Personal Expenses	$1,200	$2,000	$1,000
Estimated Total Cost of Attendance	$21,550	$48,880	$60,972
Estimated Grant / Gift Aid			
Estimated Pell Grant	$695	$695	$695
State Grant	$2,800	$500	$300
Institutional Grant	$1,500	$ 0	$45,150
Institutional Scholarship	$2,500	$15,000	$ 0
Estimated Total Grant / Gift Aid	$7,495	$16,195	$46,145
ESTIMATED NET PRICE	$14,055	$32,685	$14,827
Estimated Self-Help Aid			
Student Loan	$7,300	$5,500	$5,000
Student Work	$1,600	$ 0	$2,400
Estimated Total Self Help Aid	$8,900	$5,500	$7,400
ESTIMATED REMAINING COST	$5,155	$27,085	$7,427
Calculated Family Contribution			
Parent	$4,995	N/A	$4,995
Student	$ 0	N/A	$2,400

Additional Resources

- Links to individual college *net price* calculators -
  http://collegecost.ed.gov/netpricecenter.aspx

7 Understanding Reach, Match & Safety School Strategies

If you want to fully understand how financial aid is awarded, you need to understand the term 'preferential packaging.'

It's common for students to strategize in their college search by applying to a few *reach* schools, (*minimal chance of admission*) a few *match* schools (*likely chance of admission*), and a few *safety* schools (*high probability of admission*). But it would be financially helpful if students and families knew how 'colleges' strategize using their financial aid awards.

Colleges at almost every level of selectivity compete for students, from the few dozen highly selective colleges and universities, to the hundreds of non-selective schools.

Competing for students isn't just about filling a class. It's also about trying to bring in the strongest class, using SAT and ACT scores, GPAs, class rank, etc. And for some schools, it's also about diversity, including geography, income, gender, race, etc.

Once a class is enrolled, the school will create a *profile*, describing the average SAT and ACT scores, average high school GPA, average high school class rank, etc. The school will use the data from this *profile* to recruit the next year's class. It will also submit this data to national surveys, some of which are used to create national and regional rankings, like *U.S. News & World Report*.

So how does financial aid fit into the picture?

Schools are mindful of these rankings. Some actively attempt to move up in the rankings by improving their data. For example, if a school can attract more applicants but maintain the same class size, it could appear to be more selective. This has occurred on a number of occasions for different reasons: a school had a phenomenal football season or the school dropped the SAT or ACT requirement. Since selectivity, which is based on the percentage of students accepted, is one factor used by some of the rankings, a school could actually see a bump in their ranking the following year.

One of the more common practices these days is to use *preferential packaging*. *Preferential packaging* refers to a practice where a college will use its own money to entice and enroll students it deems more attractive and who can help strengthen its profile.

How does preferential packaging work?

Table 7A is a good example of how *preferential packaging* works. Let's say Student A applies to College X and is a top student for that school. If the college offers the student a significant scholarship, regardless of financial need, that student is more likely to enroll.

Now let's look at Student B also applying to College X who is a good student for that school, but not a top candidate. College X may offer that student a scholarship, but not as much as Student A, and may offer student loans as well.

Now let's look at Student C, also applying to College X, and who represents the lower end of the accepted student pool. College X would like to see this student enroll and help fill their class, but they're not offering Student C any scholarship money. This student may decide to enroll and may need to take out significant student loans.

Table 7A : Example of Preferential Packaging at College X		
	Annual Institutional Scholarship/Grant Amount	**Annual Loan Amount**
Accepted Student A	$35,000	$ 0
Accepted Student B	$20,000	$7,500
Accepted Student C	$ 0	$20,000

How does this tie into Reach, Match and Safety?

Using this example, College X may have been a *safety* for Student A, a *match* for Student B, and a *reach* for Student C. Looking back at Table 7A, Student A could graduate with no debt; Student B could graduate with $30,000 in student loans; and Student C *might* graduate with $80,000 in student loans.

The question these three students and their families need to answer: Is College X the right *academic* AND *financial fit* for them?

> *"Some colleges spend part of their financial aid on merit scholarships merely to improve their position in the highly publicized college rankings such as those appearing in the U.S. News & World Report." "The irony in even the most reasonable uses of tuition discounts and merit awards is that they often prove to be self-defeating. Once the first few colleges have adopted these methods, competing colleges feel compelled to do the same. The result is something of a price war in which few institutions end up gaining an advantage, since their competitors employ the same tactics."*

Source: Former Harvard President, Derek Bok,
Higher Education in America (2013)

Preferential Packaging from a Student Perspective

Rather than using the example of three students applying to one school, let's take a closer look at one student applying to three schools. In Table 7B, we're looking at Student A applying to: Reach College, Match College, and Safety College.

With the help of a school counselor, input from family and friends, and based on grades, level of courses completed (such as honors or AP), SAT and ACT scores and other factors, Student A determined which school was likely a safety, a match or a reach.

In this example, Student A is accepted to all three. In addition to federal financial aid, Student A received the following from each school:

Table 7B: Financial Aid Award Offers for Student A		
	Institutional Scholarship/Grant	Loan
Reach College	$ 0	$20,000
Match College	$20,000	$7,500
Safety College	$35,000	$ 0

Look closely and you'll see that Safety College is making it quite clear they want Student A, giving the student a $35,000 scholarship/grant. On the other hand, Reach College is making it just as clear that although they would welcome Student A to enroll, there's no scholarship/grant to support the student while enrolled.

In the next few chapters, we'll take a closer look at how students and families can be more objective in selecting between reach, match and safety schools.

BTW

There's continued debate about the cost of public vs. private colleges. It's true that the average cost of attendance at a public college is less than the average cost of a private college. However, as you see throughout these chapters, a student's net price could be lower at a private college IF the private college really wants that student. Just one more reason why it's important to understand reach, match and safety strategies.

8 Checklist of $$$ Questions for a College Search

When a consumer is looking to purchase a used car or buy a home, most look to independent inspectors to provide an objective opinion on the condition of the car or home. This process helps to better inform the consumer about the overall value or risk in making the purchase.

Given the cost of college, a similar approach is highly recommended when making a college decision. The federal government, along with student advocacy groups and others, have been pushing for more transparency so that students and families can 'look under the hood' before making a costly college decision.

There is some basic information that should be part of a well-researched college search. The information can be gathered from websites, college fairs, college visits, college representatives' visits to high schools, college interviews, school counselors and other education advisors.

The following questions should help.

What's the Price?

While this may seem like an easy question to answer, some colleges make it very difficult to find on their websites. If the website suggests you contact a representative to learn more about price, be prepared for a long and exhausting sales pitch. Proceed with caution.

Are Admissions Decisions Need-Blind?

When the admissions staff is reviewing applications, many colleges will make decisions without regard to a student's ability to pay. This is called *need-blind*. However, given the financial challenges that a growing number of colleges face, there's increasing pressure to enroll students that are considered 'full-pay,' meaning they don't need *financial aid* to enroll. You may hear a college say that they are *need-aware* or *need-sensitive*, implying that while most admissions decisions are *need-blind*, some decisions may consider a student's ability to pay.

How do private scholarships impact financial aid awards?

Thousands of students will receive private scholarships from local, regional or national organizations. They could be worth a few hundred dollars or thousands of dollars. It's important to know how a college treats these scholarships. Does the college reduce its own institutional scholarships first? Do they reduce loans first?

What's the graduation rate?

Graduation rates can be reported in a number of ways. A growing trend is to report *3-year rates* for associate's degree programs and *6-year rates* for bachelor's degree programs, though there are still plenty of students who will graduate in two years or four years in these degree programs.

Graduation rates are one objective indicator of how successful a college is with its students. There are plenty of reasons why a student might not graduate: financial, family or personal issues; desire to transfer. Table 8 provides the most recently available average graduation rates.

Note: Public community colleges typically have open enrollment, meaning anyone can enroll. That brings with it both opportunities and challenges with graduation rates, especially given the large percentage of students who need to enroll in developmental/remedial courses. If it's available, you might want to ask what the 'graduation/transfer' rate is for a better measure of success.

34

Table 8: Graduation Rates		
Type of Institution	**Rate**	**Average Graduation Rate**
4-Year Public	6-year	58.8%
4-Year Private /Nonprofit	6-year	65.1%
4-Year Private/For-profit	6-year	42.3%
2-Year Public	3-year	20.2%
2-Year Private/Nonprofit	3-year	51.0%
2-Year Private/For-Profit	3-year	61.7%
Source: U.S. Department of Education - Class of 2011		

What's the endowment?

Recall from our earlier discussion that an *endowment* represents money that a college has invested that earns interest. A percentage of this is used each year to support the college's priorities. In many cases, that includes scholarships. Knowing the size of the *endowment* will give you some indication of the financial strength of a college. Typically, the larger the *endowment*, the less dependent the college is on a student's tuition and the more it can provide in institutional aid.

For example, a college with an endowment of $1 billion could use $50 million each year to help support scholarships. However, a college with an endowment of $5 million might have only $250,000 to help support scholarships.

What percentage of alumni donates to the college?

One way of building up an endowment is to increase the percentage of alumni who donate to the institution. Institutions with greater than 40% alumni participation rate are doing very well in this arena and are usually apt to provide more institutional scholarship and/or grant money. The average donor rate for private institutions is about 20%. The average rate for public institutions is lower, closer to 10%.

Have there been any layoffs or buyouts in the past year or two?

While this may be a strange question to ask, it could be a sign that the college is tightening its belt. It could be the college didn't enroll as many students as it needed. However, it could be a sign, especially if the college has a very small *endowment*, that the belt tightening could go on for a number of years and possibly make it more difficult to get the courses you need when you need them or even the elimination of entire programs.

What's the average student debt at graduation?

How much the average student borrows to attend a specific college will give a prospective student and family an early indication of what they might face. The average undergraduate student who borrows has about $29,000 in student loans at graduation time. Proceed with caution if a school's average student debt at graduation is $40,000-$50,000.

What's the loan default rate?

A *loan default rate* is the percentage of students who graduated from a specific college with federal loans and failed to make satisfactory payments on those loans within the first three years. The national average for a loan default rate is about 14 percent.

The *loan default rate* can be a good indicator of whether graduates from a specific college are getting jobs and are able to start repaying their loans. Some schools have *loan default rates* less than one percent. At the other end of the spectrum, some schools have *loan default rates* at 25-30 percent or even higher. At a certain point, if a school continues to have a high *loan default rate*, they risk their eligibility for federal student aid.

What's the policy for transferring credits from another college?

Policies for transferring credits, either before enrolling or while enrolled, ranges from liberal to conservative. The impact can be huge for students, both in terms of time and money. Courses transferred may count toward meeting general education requirements or could be applied to meeting major/minor requirements. In many cases, some courses are accepted but won't count toward general education requirements or a student's major/minor. In this case, a student could end up graduating with more credits than necessary.

Does the institution favor first-year students over transfer students when awarding financial aid?

It's important to realize that highly publicized college-ranking publications typically emphasize data on first-year students, not transfer students. For that reason, some institutions will be more generous to first-year students with their institutional aid.

How much have costs increased over the last few years, including tuition and fees, room and board?

Whether it's a public or a private institution, knowing the trend of price increases may offer a clue to future increases. It also provides an opportunity for an institution to mention a new initiative, such as a price freeze. A price freeze typically locks in the tuition rate for a specific number of years. However, it probably doesn't lock in other costs, such as room and board.

9 Measuring the Value and Risk of Enrolling at a College

With decent information and data readily available, there's no need to buy a lemon!

When shopping for a car or house, as was mentioned in the last chapter, it's common for consumers to learn as much as they can about that specific car or that specific house. Independent car and home inspectors help consumers identify the value and risk of the car or home at a specific price.

Is it possible to measure or rate the value and risk of a specific college for a specific student at a specific price? Perhaps.

The U.S. Department of Education launched the *College Scorecard* in early 2013 as an online tool to help better inform students and families about colleges and universities. The site offers more transparency and accountability and plenty of information and data on each college. But for some students and families, it's overwhelming information.

As an independent complement to the College Scorecard, an easy-to-use, free, online tool, *CollegeValue®* was launched to help students and families determine if they're *getting a good bang for their buck.*

The website, *www.collegevalue.info*, has been compared to Kelley Blue Book. *CollegeValue®* determines if a specific college at a specific *net price* (what a student will actually pay) is a good value. To determine that, it uses three factors: *net price*, *graduation rate*, and *loan default rate*.

Net price is determined in one of three ways:

Table 9A: Determining Net Price for CollegeValue® Score			
	Option	**Description**	**Usefulness**
1	Average Net Price	A college submits this data to the U.S. Department of Education.	Good
2	Net Price from a Net Price calculator	This information is more customized because it uses a student's and a family's income and asset information.	Better
3	Actual Net Price	This information is ideal because it represents the actual net price a student will pay based on a financial aid award letter.	Best

The *graduation rate*, available using the *College Scorecard* data, is one measurable indicator of whether a college has been successful with its students.

The *loan default rate*, also available using the *College Scorecard* data, is one measurable indicator of whether or not students are getting jobs after graduation and can afford to start to pay off their student loans.

Once visitors to the site enter these three pieces of information on a specific college, they'll see a *CollegeValue® score and a rating* of Excellent, Very Good, Good, Fair or Poor. Proceed with caution if a college is rated Fair or Poor.

Table 9B: Examples of CollegeValue®			
	College A	**College B**	**College C**
Net Price	$18,000	$24,000	$32,000
Graduation Rate	88%	65%	38%
Loan Default Rate	2.2%	7.3%	13.5%
CollegeValue® Score*	23	43	98
CollegeValue® Rating	Excellent	Good	Poor
* The lower the score, the better the value			

Just like the Kelley Blue Book is for cars, the purpose of the *CollegeValue®* site and its customized rating is to provide simple, but important information to students and families BEFORE they make costly decisions. Would it be helpful if students and families knew in advance that a specific college had a low graduation rate and a high loan default rate? It should! Who wants to buy a lemon?

Additional Resources

- CollegeValue® –
  www.collegevalue.info

- College Scorecard –
  http://collegecost.ed.gov/scorecard/

10 FAFSA and CSS/PROFILE

Almost 20 million students are enrolled in college these days; most of them will have filed the FAFSA...and survived!

Parents may or may not turn out for teacher/parent nights at a high school these days, but offer a workshop on how to file the *Free Application for Federal Student Aid (FAFSA)* and the auditorium is packed! There is so much information and detail available on the FAFSA, that it can be overwhelming. The following are some highlights about filing the FAFSA.

FAFSA

- It's the required form to determine eligibility for federal financial aid and most college scholarships. This is the START of the process.

- The FAFSA determines the *Expected Family Contribution (EFC)* - the dollar amount a family is expected to contribute per year toward the *cost of attendance*.

- **Pay attention to deadlines**; too many students miss out on 'money' because they missed the deadlines for filing the FAFSA. Note that deadlines for state aid that require the FAFSA may be earlier than an institution's deadline.

- Driven primarily by parents' and students' incomes, assets, and number of students in college.

- Should be filed online whenever possible using *FAFSA on the Web* (FOTW).

- Filing online requires a Personal Identification Number (PIN) for both students and parents; your PIN serves as your electronic signature.

- PINs must be obtained in advance of actually filing the FAFSA.

- Filing online allows you to use an interactive *data retrieval tool* that takes you to an IRS website and allows you to transfer some of your tax return data.

- Filed after January 1 for the upcoming school year.

- Once filed, a student will receive a *Student Aid Report (SAR)*.

- Once filed, the colleges listed will receive an *Institutional Student Information Record (ISIR)*. Students are advised to <u>list their colleges in alphabetical order</u>. Colleges have been known to assume that the order in which colleges are listed on the FAFSA indicates a student's preferences; financial aid awards have been impacted, and not always in a student's favor.

- Some students will be selected for '*verification*,' which is a request for additional documentation to 'verify' the data submitted.

CSS/PROFILE

Another financial aid form some students will need to file is the College Board's *College Scholarship Service (CSS)/PROFILE*.

- About 250 undergraduate colleges require the CSS/PROFILE, looking for additional financial information to distribute institutional aid.

- Available only online.

- Pre-Application worksheet will save you a lot of time.

- Automatic fee waiver for eligible students.

44

- Registrations are accepted beginning October 1 of the year before a student intends to start college.
- Filers will receive an online Acknowledgement/Data Confirmation Report.

Other Forms

In addition to the FAFSA and CSS/PROFILE, some students, depending on where they live and what schools they apply to, will be required to complete additional financial aid forms.

BTW

Some higher income families may wonder if it's worth their time and effort to file the *FAFSA*, knowing they are not eligible for need-based aid. If they're interested in federal loans that are not income-eligible and may offer lower interest rates, they should still file the *FAFSA*. Also, some institutions may require it for merit-based awards.

Additional Resources
- FAFSA –
  www.fafsa.ed.gov
- Personal Identification Number (PIN) –
  www.pin.ed.gov
- CSS/PROFILE –
  http://student.collegeboard.org/css-financial-aid-profile

11 Financial Aid Comparison Tool

You would think receiving a *financial aid award letter* would bring clarity about what a family will have to pay. Unfortunately, and all too often, the award letter not only lacks clarity, it can also be misleading.

For example, there have been award letters that omit certain *cost of attendance* items, such as transportation, books and supplies, or other educational expenses. Or, the letter suggests that your *net price* (what a student will actually pay) is calculated after subtracting scholarships, grants *and* loans. That's wrong. As was pointed out in the beginning chapters, *net price is the cost of attendance minus scholarships and grants, NOT loans*. How a student and family pay the *net price* <u>might</u> include loans.

The federal government has been working on addressing this and has introduced the *Financial Aid Shopping Sheet*. This form was designed to standardize and simplify financial aid award letters. It includes:

- Cost of attendance
- Grants and scholarships
- Net price
- Options to pay net price, including self-help aid like loans and work-study

To date, more than 2,000 colleges and universities have agreed to use this format. Table 11A depicts how financial aid awards can be compared using this new template for financial aid award letters.

Note: The template from the U.S. Department of Education encourages colleges to include their graduation rate and loan default rate as well. Unfortunately, because the form is 'voluntary,' don't expect schools with low graduation rates and high loan default rates to embrace those components! But you can find them at the College Scorecard.

Table 11A shows how beneficial it is to students and families to review financial aid awards side-by-side, using the new Financial Aid Shopping Sheet format.

Table 11A: Example: Comparison of Financial Aid Awards			
	College A	College B	College C
Costs in the 2014-15 Year			
Estimated Cost of Attendance	**$21,550**	**$48,880**	**$60,972**
Tuition and fees	$8,080	$32,760	$46,088
Housing and meals	$9,520	$11,960	$12,884
Books and supplies	$2,000	$960	$1,000
Transportation	$750	$1,200	$0
Other education costs	$1,200	$2,000	$1,000
Grants and scholarships to pay for college			
Total Grants and Scholarships *('Gift' aid; no repayment needed)*	**$7,495**	**$16,195**	**$46,145**
Grants and scholarships from your school	$4,000	$15,000	$45,150
Federal Pell Grant	$695	$695	$695
Grants from your state	$2,800	$500	$300
Other scholarships you can use	$0	$0	$0
What you will pay for college			
Net Price/Costs	**$14,055**	**$32,685**	**$14,827**
(Cost of attendance minus total grants and scholarships)			

Table 11A: Example: Comparison of Financial Aid Awards	College A	College B	College C
Options to pay net price/costs			
Work Options			
Work-Study (Federal, state or institutional)	$1,600	$ 0	$2,400
Loan Options*			
Federal Perkins Loan	$ 0	$ 0	$ 0
Federal Direct Subsidized Loan	$3,500	$3,500	$3,500
Federal Direct Unsubsidized Loan	$3,800	$2,000	$1,500
* Recommended amounts shown here. You may be eligible for a different amount. Contact your financial aid office.			
Other Options			
Family Contribution *(As calculated by the institution using information reported on the FAFSA or to your institution)*	**$4,995**	**$4,995**	**$7,395**
Payment plan offered by the institution			
Parent or Graduate PLUS Loans			
Military and/or National Service benefits			
Non-federal private education loan			
Graduation Rate	51.7%	26.9%	90.8%
Loan Default Rate	7.1%	13.8%	2.2%

Based on the actual financial aid awards, it's also helpful to take one more step and calculate the *CollegeValue®* for each institution to see what kind of *bang for your buck* you're getting.

Table 11B: CollegeValue® Ratings	
College A	Very Good
College B	Poor
College C	Excellent

From a *financial fit* perspective, College C appears to be the front-runner, even though it has the highest *cost of attendance*. Its *CollegeValue® rating* of *Excellent* reflects a lower *net price* (what a student will actually pay), high *graduation rate* and low *loan default rate*. College A is a good runner up. College B could be a little too risky.

Additional Resources

- Financial Aid Shopping Sheet – www2.ed.gov/policy/highered/guid/aid-offer/index.html

- CollegeValue® – www.collegevalue.info

- Financial Aid Office that sent the award letter

12 Loans: How to Borrow

Students should thoroughly understand the short- and long-term impact of borrowing BEFORE they make a final college decision.

Given the cost of college, including both undergraduate and graduate schools, most students will end up borrowing to help cover costs. Before students make final decisions on which colleges to attend, they should thoroughly understand the short- and long-term impact of their borrowing.

Types of Loans

As you learned in Chapter 4, the following table highlights the types of loans currently available to students and parents. Some distinctions worth noting are:

- In most cases, federal loans carry lower interest rates than private loans and should be included before considering private loans.
- The difference between *subsidized* and *unsubsidized* loans has to do with the interest accruing while a student is in school. For *subsidized* loans, the federal government pays the interest while a student is enrolled. For *unsubsidized* loans, the interest is just added to the total amount owed. Include all subsidized options when possible.

Table 12A: Types of Loans	
Federal Direct Subsidized Stafford Loan	• Must be repaid with interest • Based on financial need • Maximum amount: $3,500 -$5,500 per year • Interest is paid by government while in school (*subsidized*) • Student is the borrower
Federal Direct Unsubsidized Stafford Loan	• Must be repaid with interest • No requirement to demonstrate financial need • College determines maximum amount • Interest accrues while in college (*unsubsidized*) • Student is the borrower
Federal Perkins Loan	• Must be repaid with interest • Students must show significant financial need • Maximum award: $5,500 per year • Administered by a college's financial aid office • Deadlines vary by college • Student is the borrower
Direct PLUS Loan	• Must be repaid with interest • Maximum amounts vary • Requires a credit check • U.S. Dept. of Education is the lender • Parent is the borrower
Private	• Must be repaid with interest • Maximum amount varies • Issued by a lender such as a bank or credit union • Parent or student is the borrower

How much is reasonable to borrow?

There has been much media attention paid to the more than $1 trillion in student debt. The question each student and family needs to address is how much debt is affordable and appropriate. Before you do that, it would be helpful for students to understand their personal budgets for *after* they've completed all of their schooling. Estimating your anticipated annual salary will definitely help to determine a reasonable amount to borrow for college.

Budget Now

Deciding to take out student loans is a long-term financial commitment, potentially lasting 20 years or more. All too often, high school students make decisions on loan amounts that will determine their quality of life for years, such as living on their own or living with parents. But what if students worked backwards and determined their post-college/graduate-school quality of life *first* and then allowed that to determine how much they're willing to borrow?

One recommended approach to personal budgeting uses a formula credited to now Senator Elizabeth Warren and her daughter Amelia Warren Tyagi, called the 50/30/20 budget. It basically breaks down to include:

- 50% of after-tax pay for fixed expenses/needs

- 30% of after-tax pay for discretionary expenses/wants

- 20% of after-tax pay for financial commitments

Table 12B: 50/30/20 Budget Example		
Annual Salary	$45,000	
Monthly (after taxes)	$2,800	
1. Needs (50%)		
Housing, transportation, utilities, food, etc.		
Subtotal	$1,400	50%
2. Wants (30%)		
Entertainment, gym fees, hobbies, pets, personal care, restaurants, shopping, etc.		
Subtotal	$840	30%
3. Financial Commitments (20%)		
Student loans, savings and retirement contributions		
Subtotal	$560	20%

Table 12B above demonstrates this budget approach using a new graduate with a starting salary of $45,000.

This worthwhile exercise makes some assumptions about what an individual might define as 'needs' or 'wants' and commitments to certain financial obligations and goals. To make this a worthwhile tool and exercise for those considering how

53

much to borrow, the 20 percent for financial commitments is a good starting point.

Based on the 50/30/20 example, this graduate has about $560 available each month for 'financial commitments.' Keep in mind that this category includes student loan payments as well as savings and retirement contributions. *Reality check: That $560 may have to help cover a second student loan for a young couple living on one income*!

> **10 percent of monthly after-tax pay is a reasonable student loan payment.**

In this example, 10 percent of after-tax pay would be about $280 toward a student loan payment. As Table 12C shows, this individual could be looking at borrowing up to $26,500 and still be in good shape financially. Keep in mind, the $26,500 is the total amount borrowed, so if a student is planning on graduate school, that total may need to be split between undergraduate and graduate school.

Table 12C: Reasonable Borrowing (*estimates only*)			
Proposed Annual Salary	**Monthly After-Tax Pay (*Estimate*)**	**10% Student Loan Payment**	**Reasonable Total Amount to Borrow***
$30,000	$1,875	$188	$17,500
$45,000	$2,800	$280	$26,500
$60,000	$3,750	$375	$35,500
			* Based on 5% interest rate

Armed with this type of information, students and families can be better informed and prepared to make borrowing decisions.

Additional Resources

- Federal Student Loans – http://studentaid.ed.gov/

- *All Your Worth: The Ultimate Lifetime Money Plan* (2005); Elizabeth Warren and Amelia Warren Tyagi

13 Loans: How to Repay

Knowing how much to borrow for college expenses is key to a student's future quality of life. Understanding what options a student will have to repay those loans can also impact a student's future quality of life.

Repayment Plans

The U.S. Department of Education assigns *federal student loans to a loan servicer* who then handles all the billing. There are several repayment plans to chose from:

- *Standard Repayment Plan* – Automatically assigned to borrowers unless they choose another plan; payments are fixed and paid over 10 years.

- *Graduated Repayment Plan* – Payments start out low and increase every two years; made for up to 10 years.

- *Extended Repayment Plan* – Payments can be fixed or graduated; made for up to 25 years.

- *Income-Based Repayment Plan (IBR)* – Designed for those who have a partial financial hardship; payments are based on income and family size; amount is 15 percent of discretionary income; made over a period of 25 years.

- *Pay as You Earn Repayment Plan* – Designed for those who have a partial financial hardship; based on income and family size; adjusted each year; made over a period of 20 years.

- *Income-Contingent Repayment Plan* – Payments are calculated each year and are based on income, family size, and the total amount owed on direct loans; made for up to 25 years.

- *Income-Sensitive Repayment Plan* – Payments increase or decrease based on annual income and are made for a maximum period of 10 years.

Note: Not all federal loans qualify for all repayment plans. The lender dictates private loan repayment options.

Loan Forgiveness or Discharge

There are a number of opportunities or circumstances that allow for student loans to be forgiven, canceled or discharged:

- *Teacher Loan Forgiveness* – Borrowers must have been teaching full-time in a low-income public or nonprofit private elementary or secondary school for five consecutive years; as much as $17,500 of your subsidized or unsubsidized loans may be forgiven.

- *Public Service Loan Forgiveness* – Borrowers must be employed full-time by a public service organization AND have made 120 loan payments to be eligible. Public service organizations include: Federal, State, local or Tribal agencies; public child or family service agencies; nonprofit 501(c)(3) organizations; private organizations offering eligible public services like emergency management, public safety and others.

Note: Some repayment plans, including Income-Based, Pay as You Earn, and Income-Contingent, provide loan forgiveness if borrowers have a balance owed after 20-25 years of making payments.

In addition to these forgiveness options, loans can be discharged in the case of total and permanent disability or death.

It's important to know that student loans are seldom discharged in bankruptcy.

Returning to College When a Student Has Defaulted on a Loan

For a host of reasons, some students will fail to make their scheduled student loan payments and will end up defaulting on these loans. Eventually, circumstances change and some of the students who defaulted will want to return to college. Could they be eligible for financial aid again? Possibly.

The federal government offers a one-time-only opportunity for borrowers to regain eligibility for federal financial aid. It's referred to as *rehabilitating a defaulted loan.*

The process entails the borrower making agreed-upon reasonable and affordable payments for an agreed-upon number of months. Once the payments have been made and a lender has purchased the loan, the borrower should have the same benefits as others in good standing, including qualifying for federal financial aid and deferring the loan payments once enrolled in school.

Convicted Felons

Over the years, I've had the opportunity to work with men who had spent time in prison. Some of them were interested in turning their lives around and continuing their education.

'Word on the street' for these men and women who have been incarcerated was that they couldn't qualify for federal financial aid because they were convicted felons. That's not necessarily true.

Question #23 on the FAFSA asks:

> *Have you been convicted for the possession or sale of illegal drugs for an offense that occurred **while you were receiving federal student aid** (such as grants, loans or work-study)?*

Note that it says, "while you were receiving federal student aid." In other words, if an individual were convicted for possession or sale of illegal drugs while not receiving federal student aid, they answer NO.

Note also that the FAFSA does not ask about convictions for other types of crimes.

If an individual was convicted for the possession or sale of illegal drugs while receiving federal financial aid, the FAFSA directions say:

Answer "Yes," but complete and submit this application, and we will mail you a worksheet to help you determine if your conviction affects your eligibility for aid.

The individual will receive a Student Aid Eligibility Worksheet for Question 23 along with the Student Aid Report (SAR). The worksheet will help to determine when the individual will be eligible for federal financial aid again.

BTW

Applying for a loan consolidation may be worth considering. Direct Consolidation Loans permit Federal education loan borrowers to have just one lender and one monthly bill as well as flexible repayment options. They may even lower the borrower's overall monthly payment. There are options to consolidate private loans as well. As a rule of thumb, federal loans should not be consolidated with private loans.

Additional Resources
- Federal Student Loans – www.studentaid.ed.gov

14 Alternatives to Earning Traditional College Credits

Colleges and universities typically operate on a course *credit* system. For example, a student taking a semester-long course would earn a number of credits. Many times a course will carry three credits, perhaps more if there is a laboratory requirement.

In order to be awarded a *certificate* or *degree* from a college, usually a specific number of credits must be earned. For example:

- Certificate – Could be as few as 10 credits or more than 60

- Associate's Degree – Typically 60 credits

- Bachelor's Degree – Typically 120 credits

Given the growing cost of college, students and families would benefit from knowing what additional opportunities exist to earn college credits and thus potentially reduce the time and money it would take to complete a program or degree. Without exaggeration, *the potential savings could be in years and tens of thousands of dollars.*

The following represent some of the more popular programs, including *credit-by-exam*, which can lead to college credits and save significant time and money.

Dual Enrollment

Dual enrollment allows high school students to enroll in college-level courses, in many cases, either free or at a reduced price. Some credits count toward both high school graduation requirements and a college degree. Students usually need to have a minimum GPA to qualify and have the consent of their high school and parent(s).

> *According to a 2013 report from the National Center for Education Statistics (NCES), more than 1.2 million high school students took courses for college credit within a dual enrollment program. Of that number, about 70% were enrolled at 2-year public colleges.*

Note: Federal financial aid is not available for dual enrollment.

Advanced Placement (AP) Courses

For high school students prepared for more rigorous course work, the College Board's Advanced Placement (AP) courses offer a great opportunity to earn college credit. Following the completion of the course, students take an AP exam, which is scored on a 1-5 scale, with 5 being the highest. Typically, a college will grant college credit and/or placement into an upper-level course for a score of 5 or 4, though many colleges will also offer credit and/or placement into an upper-level course for a score of 3. Each college determines its own credit-awarding policies for AP exam score requirements. Students should inquire about a college's requirements while conducting their college search.

> *A student could save $3,000 or more on college costs for each high-scored AP exam.*

More than 30 AP courses are available, including:

- Art History
- Biology
- Calculus AB
- Calculus BC
- Chemistry
- Chinese Language and Culture
- Computer Science A
- English Language and Composition
- English Literature and Composition
- Environmental Science
- European History
- French Language and Culture
- German Language and Culture
- Government and Politics: Comparative
- Government and Politics: United States
- Human Geography
- Italian Language and Culture
- Japanese Language and Culture
- Latin
- Macroeconomics
- Microeconomics
- Music Theory
- Physics B
- Physics C: Electricity and Magnetism
- Physics C: Mechanics
- Psychology
- Spanish Language and Culture
- Spanish Literature and Culture

- Statistics
- Studio Art: 2-D Design
- Studio Art: 3-D Design
- Studio Art: Drawing
- United States History
- World History

Whether a high school offers AP courses and how many seems to be determined by student demand and funding. In the end, taking AP courses could save time and money and influence college admissions decisions.

International Baccalaureate (IB)

The International Baccalaureate (IB) program, sponsored by the International Baccalaureate Organization, is offered in more than 130 countries, including about 800 high schools in the United States. If a student chooses to participate in the IB program, they have two options:

- *IB Diploma* – Students take all IB courses during their junior and senior years.
- *IB Certificate* – Students take individual IB courses and earn a certificate for each successfully completed class.

IB courses are either *standard level* or *higher level*. Final exams for each course are scored 1-7, with 7 being the highest. *Diploma* students must take at least 3 higher-level courses and earn at least 24 points (based on exam scores of 1-7) to receive an IB diploma.

Each college determines its own credit-awarding policies for IB exam score requirements. Students should inquire about a college's requirements while conducting their college search.

> *Some colleges will grant sophomore status to high school students who complete the IB Diploma. That could save $40,000 or more and a year's worth of study for a student who plans to attend a private, 4-year college.*

College Level Examination Program (CLEP)

Developed by the College Board, CLEP has been around for more than 40 years. Exams test mastery in specific subjects. How the exam taker acquired the knowledge could range from work or life experience, course work from years ago, or more recently, from the growing number of free, Massive Open Online Courses (MOOCs) or other free, online courses.

There are over 1,800 test centers that administer the CLEP exams. More than 2,900 colleges and universities grant college credit based on CLEP exam scores.

CLEP offers 33 exams in five subject areas:

Business

- Financial Accounting
- Information Systems and Computer Applications
- Introductory Business Law
- Principles of Management
- Principles of Marketing

Composition & Literature

- American Literature
- Analyzing and Interpreting Literature
- College Composition
- College Composition Modular
- English Literature
- Humanities

History and Social Sciences

- American Government
- History of the United States I: Early Colonization to 1877
- History of the United States II: 1865 to the Present
- Human Growth and Development
- Introduction to Educational Psychology
- Introductory Psychology

- Introductory Sociology
- Principles of Macroeconomics
- Principles of Microeconomics
- Social Sciences and History
- Western Civilization I: Ancient Near East to 1648
- Western Civilization II: 1648 to the Present

Science & Mathematics
- Biology
- Calculus
- Chemistry
- College Algebra
- College Mathematics
- Natural Sciences
- Pre-calculus

World Languages
- French – Levels 1 and 2
- German – Levels 1 and 2
- Spanish – Levels 1 and 2

By passing a CLEP exam, students can earn 3-12 college credits. Exams cost $80.

CLEP exams are ideal for adult students looking to return to college for a certificate or degree, potentially reducing the cost and time to complete a certificate or degree.

There seems to be a growing sentiment that high school students who have taken rigorous courses are also turning to the CLEP to reduce future college costs and potentially graduate early. For example, a student who has studied Spanish for four years in high school might be able to sit for the Spanish CLEP exam and earn 3-12 credits. That's real time and money saved!

According to a study conducted by the Council of Adult and Experiential Learning (CAEL), students

> **who *took CLEP exams to earn bachelor's degrees saved between 2.5 and 10.1 months of time in earning their degrees, compared to students that did not take prior learning assessments* such as *CLEP*.**

DSST (formerly DANTES Subject Standardized Tests)

While CLEP exams are designed to measure competencies for lower-level college courses, DSST exams are available for both upper- and lower-level credit. Originally designated for military personnel only, DSST exams are now available to anyone wanting to earn *credits-by-exam*.

DSST offers 38 exams in six subject areas:

Business

- Business Law II
- Business Mathematics
- Human Resource Management
- Introduction to Business
- Introduction to Computing
- Management Information Systems
- Money and Banking
- Organizational Behavior
- Personal Finance
- Principles of Finance
- Principles of Financial Accounting
- Principles of Supervision

Humanities

- Ethics in America
- Introduction to World Religions
- Principles of Public Speaking

Math

- Fundamentals of College Algebra
- Principles of Statistics

Physical Science

- Astronomy
- Here's to Your Health
- Environment and Humanity
- Physical Geology
- Principles of Physical Science I

Social Sciences

- A History of the Vietnam War
- Art of the Western World
- The Civil War and Reconstruction
- Criminal Justice
- Foundations of Education
- Fundamentals of Counseling
- General Anthropology
- Human/Cultural Geography
- Introduction to Law Enforcement
- Introduction to the Modern Middle East
- Life-Span Developmental Psychology
- Rise and Fall of the Soviet Union
- Substance Abuse
- Western Europe since 1945

Technology

- Technical Writing

DSST exams are administered at more than 1,200 test centers on college campuses and military bases, with more than 2,000 colleges awarding college credits for qualifying scores.

Challenge Exam

In addition to CLEP and DSST, a number of colleges will allow a student to 'challenge' a course if the student feels confident that he/she already has mastered the content of that course. Challenge exams are usually at the discretion of a faculty member. Each college determines its own credit-awarding policies and prices for challenge exam score requirements. Students should inquire about a college's requirements while conducting their college search.

Additional Resources

- Advanced Placement (AP) –
  https://apstudent.collegeboard.org/home

- International Baccalaureate (IB) –
  www.ibo.org/

- College Level Examination Program (CLEP) –
  http://clep.collegeboard.org/

- DSST –
  http://getcollegecredit.com/

15 Reducing the Need for Remedial Classes

Imagine a recent high school graduate who sits for a placement exam for college, only to discover that he or she did not score high enough to place into college-level math or English. For countless reasons, millions of recent high school graduates and adults find themselves underprepared to tackle college-level work and are in need of remedial or developmental courses. Such courses seldom carry college credit and eat away at financial aid eligibility.

> *By some estimates, as many as 25 percent of first-time students at 4-year colleges and some 70 percent at 2-year community colleges require remedial or developmental courses.*

As if those figures weren't discouraging enough, the data show that the chances of completing a certificate or degree diminish with each remedial class taken by a student.

Some high schools are addressing this issue by having their juniors sit for college placement exams and use the results to determine appropriate courses for their senior year. For example, high school juniors who score low in math may enroll in an appropriate fourth-year math course their senior year, strengthen their math skills and be better prepared to place into college-level math right out of high school.

Of course, not everyone has the luxury of enrolling in a yearlong course before taking the placement exam. This is particularly true of adult students who may not have had a math class in more than a decade.

Most experts who work with students taking placement exams emphasize the need (and wisdom) to put some real effort into reviewing the materials before sitting for the exam. Sometimes just spending a few weeks reviewing the materials in advance can make a difference in placing into college-level courses. Or rather than two levels of remedial work, maybe only one level of remedial work is needed.

Unfortunately, over the years I've heard one story after another of students who rushed into student advising centers and insisted that they had to take the placement exam right then because their very busy schedules didn't permit returning to campus yet again. I would caution students that such rash decisions could have dire consequences. Once again, that's time and money!

Additional Resources

- ACCUPLACER –
  http://accuplacer.collegeboard.org/students

- ACT Compass – www.act.org/compass/

16 Stackable Credentials

Historically, there has been a push to provide access to college to all who desired it. High schools and adult education programs have been geared to help students become college ready. Today, we're more apt to hear about efforts that focus not just on 'access,' but on retention and successful completion as well.

The push to increase retention and graduation rates is due, in part, to the demands of the labor market that requires a well-educated workforce, especially in a knowledge-based economy. Obtaining the appropriate education and credentials can certainly help to provide more employment options and financial security for individuals.

The challenge for some students is the time, stamina and money it takes to earn a degree. Yet without some type of additional credential beyond high school, many will be tied to low-wage jobs with very little opportunity for advancement.

There has been a push by a number of industries, including advanced manufacturing, energy, healthcare and information technology, to partner with colleges and create short-, mid- and long-term education pathways to help meet their workforce needs. These growing partnerships have led to the creation of what is being referred to as 'stackable credentials.'

For example, the energy industries in Texas and North Carolina have partnered with their state's community colleges to create certificate programs to help meet the demand for specific entry-level energy jobs. Students/employees who complete the certificate programs can return at any point to take the next level certificate and potentially advance their career. Many, if not all of the credits acquired along the way, could be applied to an associate's degree.

The stackable credential approach has some real advantages. Some students are looking for a quick entry into the job market. This could help. Some students are not in a position to commit to a degree program. Again, this could help.

Given the high number of students who initially fail to complete an associate's degree, the stackable credential approach may be ideal for some. Rather than biting off more than they can chew, it could provide an early win for students and lay the groundwork for continuing their education as time and motivation permit.

17 Reverse Transfer

In an effort to increase college graduation rates, particularly at the community college level, a relatively new trend is gaining traction. It's called *reverse transfer*.

At first glance, *reverse transfer* would simply suggest students transferring from a 4-year college to a 2-year college and earning their associate's degree from the 2-year college. The new trend is much more than that.

- The process starts with carefully crafted *articulation agreements* between 2-year and 4-year institutions.

- It targets students who have transferred from a 2-year to a 4-year institution **before** earning a degree and who typically have completed 12-45 credits at the 2-year institution.

- It requires strong communication between the interested student and the two institutions to ensure all the requirements are met.

- Students are awarded the associate's degree upon completion of the remaining required courses taken while attending the 4-year institution.

- Students continue at the 4-year institution toward the bachelor's degree.

There are significant benefits to *reverse transfer*:

- More students complete an associate's degree, even if they don't complete the bachelor's degree.

- The community colleges realize an increase in their graduation rates.

Thousands of students choose a community college as a stepping-stone to obtaining a bachelor's degree. Unfortunately, far too many of these students who transfer **before** completing their associate's degree are also unable to complete the bachelor's degree. *Reverse transfer* provides an opportunity to at least award the associate's degree. That way, should a student need to 'stop out' from the 4-year program, they enter the job market with a credential that can provide more career and financial opportunities than no degree at all.

BTW

While some students may choose community colleges to strengthen their college readiness skills, others may choose them for their outstanding programs. Given the soaring costs of a college education, there appears to be an increased interest in enrolling at community colleges to save money as well. If students are considering continuing on to a 4-year institution, they should inquire about existing articulation agreements between the community college and 4-year colleges. Strong articulation agreements could save students time and money.

18 Too Many Credits

Perhaps nothing adds more to the cost of a college education than extra credits!

In Chapter 14, we discussed typical credit requirements for degrees:

- Associate's Degree – typically 60 credits
- Bachelor's Degree – typically 120 credits

Yet, according to Complete College America, a national nonprofit:

- Associate's degree-seeking students, on average, earned 81 credits instead of the more typical 60.
- Bachelor's degree-seeking students, on average, earned 135 credits instead of the more typical 120.

There's a host of reasons why a student might exceed the required number of credits for a degree: change of major, a need to complete prerequisites, transfer to another institution, or even personal interest. Some may even take courses that are not required in order to meet financial aid eligibility. Yet most students may not be aware of the significant cost-increase tied to their decisions.

> *The 21 additional credits at a community college, on average, would cost about $2,300. The 15 additional credits at a 4-year private college, on average, could cost about $15,000!*

Add the additional cost for books, housing, transportation, and then factor in the additional time, not just in semesters, but potentially in years, and you can see how this is a major issue of time and money!

There's no easy answer or quick fix for this. However, to help minimize this costly path, students could benefit from *registering for their classes as early as possible*. All too often, students are shut out of required courses. This may be due to late registration or possible budget cuts. Registering as early as possible each semester might help.

Students exploring a change of major should speak with their advisors and *craft a semester-by-semester course plan*. Doing so might help to identify potential problems to completing the degree on time, such as a required course offered only once a year, or a proposed change in program requirements.

Students planning to transfer should *consult with the colleges to which they are considering transferring*. They should inquire about whether certain courses they're planning to take that semester or year will transfer **and** count toward their degree requirements at the new college.

BTW

Students may risk federal financial aid eligibility if they're not making satisfactory academic progress toward a degree as determined by their institution's policies. Also worth noting is that some public institutions may impose a tuition surcharge to students who exceed the semester credit hour limit of their program.

Additional Resources
- Student aid eligibility –
  http://studentaid.ed.gov/eligibility/staying-eligible

19 Competency-Based Learning

Is competency-based learning the ultimate solution for saving time and money?

Previous chapters have discussed *credit-by-exam* and other alternatives to earning traditional college credits. As higher education evolves to meet the growing demands of a knowledge-based economy, so do the education pathways designed to meet those growing demands.

You've probably been hearing more and more about *competency-based programs*. And as more colleges and programs receive approvals from accrediting agencies and the U.S. Department of Education, you'll hear even more. What are they and just exactly how are they already challenging the *status quo*?

The standard for measuring what a student learns in college has typically been tied to the *credit hour* and what some have called 'seat time' in a classroom. For example, a student enrolls in a 3-credit course, follows a course syllabus, participates in classroom instruction for 14 weeks, completes homework assignments and is tested to prove knowledge acquired in the subject.

In essence, a faculty member has determined what the learning outcomes should be for the students enrolled in the class. Or, in other words, what competencies students should be able to demonstrate by the end of the course.

But is 'seat time' in the classroom (or online) the only way to acquire competencies? As was noted in earlier chapters, some students have acquired a body of knowledge in a specific subject from various learning experiences, including work, free online courses, personal reading, etc.

Frustrated and discouraged by rising college costs, students and families are more actively exploring ways to control those costs yet still be able to demonstrate, typically to an employer, that they have the necessary competencies to do the job. Thus the stage has been set to help meet students' and families' needs using an alternative education pathway.

While a few schools have been offering competency-based programs for a while, like Western Governors University, it seems it wasn't until Southern New Hampshire University received approval from the U.S. Department of Education in 2013 that the movement gained momentum.

How does competency-based learning work?

A competency-based program provides an opportunity for students to capitalize on previous learning experiences and prove through *direct assessment* what they already know. *Direct assessment* can take many forms, including exams, portfolios, performances, etc.

What is the real advantage for students? There's no wasting time and money taking required courses when they have already acquired the necessary competencies in that subject and can demonstrate that knowledge through some form of direct assessment.

In establishing the criteria institutions would need to follow to be eligible for federal student aid, the U.S. Department of Education, in its March 2013 letter to colleges, noted:

> *Competency-based approaches to education have the potential for assuring the quality and extent of learning, shortening the time to degree/certificate completion, developing stackable credentials that ease student transitions between school and work,*

and reducing the overall cost of education for both career-technical and degree programs.

It's worth noting, however, that competency-based learning and its self-paced approach is not for everyone. It requires real discipline and sustained motivation. For now, most programs appear to be targeting the adult student, but it may have long-term impacts for traditional-age students as well.

It's quite possible that a few years down the road, an employer will ask job candidates to prove their competencies for a specific position during the screening process. How the student acquired those competencies, whether through a degree program or alternate education pathway, will be of little interest to the employer.

Additional Resources

- U.S. Dept. of Education on Competency-based programs – http://ifap.ed.gov/dpcletters/GEN1310.html

20 Final Thoughts

As I mentioned in the very beginning, students and families can't control the cost of college, but they can control how much they spend. The reality is we've reached a tipping point with college costs that requires a more savvy approach to college spending.

Saving for college is still important, but most families may not be able to save enough to cover the *net price* (what a student actually pays). The federal government and colleges are slowly attempting to make important and necessary information available to the public so that students and families can make more informed decisions.

Online tools such as estimators for expected family contributions as well as net price and CollegeValue® calculators are helping thousands of students and families navigate this daunting process.

Being aware of accumulating credits in the most efficient and cost-effective manner can make a huge difference in time and money. And knowing how much to borrow in relation to future anticipated earnings would help graduates become more financially independent.

In the end, it's up to students and families to do their homework and ask questions until they're confident their final college choices are both good academic *and* financial fits.

Glossary

529 Plan - A qualified tuition program typically set up by a state or eligible educational institution that allows a family to either prepay or contribute to an account established for paying a student's qualified education expenses at an eligible educational institution.

Academic Fit - A college match that considers a student's academic achievements and interests.

Accrued Interest - Interest added to a loan on a daily basis.

Adjusted Gross Income (AGI) - Total income after allowable deductions.

Advanced Placement (AP) Program - Rigorous courses offered to students at participating high schools; high scores on the AP exam may qualify students for college credits and/or placement into upper-level college courses; offered through The College Board.

American College Testing (ACT) Program - One of several standardized tests that may be taken by students planning to gain admission into college; offered by ACT, a nonprofit organization.

American Opportunity Credit - An IRS-approved tax credit of up to $2,500 per student based on income; can be claimed for only four tax years.

Articulation Agreement - A contract between two or more institutions usually designed to provide additional academic options for students.

Automatic Zero EFC - A designation for when specific income-driven requirements are met when filing the FAFSA, resulting in a $0 Expected Family Contribution (EFC); requires an Adjusted Gross Income of $24,000 or less.

Award Letter - Letter for an accepted/enrolled student detailing the types and amounts of financial aid being offered.

Campus-Based Aid - Monies received by an institution from the federal government to be used for financially needy students; includes Perkins loans, Supplemental Education Opportunity Grants (SEOG), and Work-Study.

Challenge Exam - An assessment that allows students to demonstrate competency in a specific subject without having to take the course.

Chivas Regal Effect - The perception that a higher-priced institution is better than a lower-priced one.

College Level Examination Program (CLEP) - Exams designed to measure a student's competency in a specific subject matter; qualifying exam scores result in college credits awarded by participating institutions; program is offered through The College Board.

College Scholarship Service (CSS)/PROFILE - A financial aid form used by more than 250 colleges to distribute institutional aid; requires more financial information than was provided on the FAFSA

College Scorecard - An online tool created and maintained by the U.S. Department of Education that provides useful data on thousands of colleges and universities.

CollegeValue® Score - An online tool that provides a measure of the value and risk associated with enrolling at a specific college at a specific price.

Competency-Based Education - An approach to education that allows student learning to be self-paced with direct assessment measuring knowledge acquired.

Cost of Attendance (COA) - The price for tuition and fees, room and board, books and supplies, transportation and other educational expenses for a term or academic year.

Coverdell Education Savings Accounts (ESA) - A college savings plan offered by banks and other IRS-approved entities.

Credit-by-Exam - A direct assessment of a student's knowledge in a specific subject/course; serves as an alternative to taking the actual course; examples include CLEP, DSST and challenge exams.

Data Retrieval Tool - An online IRS tool that allows FAFSA filers to transfer some of their tax return data to the FAFSA form.

Default - Student loans enter default status when payments are past due for a specified period of time; each loan's promissory note specifies its default timeframe.

Deferment - One way to postpone repayment of a student loan if a student meets certain conditions; for subsidized loans, the federal government pays interest during this period.

Delinquency - A designation used when a borrower fails to make a full scheduled loan payment on time.

Demonstrated Need - The cost of attendance minus the expected family contribution.

Dependent Students - Students who derive significant financial support from their families and don't meet the criteria for independent student.

Direct Assessment - A way of measuring a student's knowledge in a specific subject or course, including exams, research papers, projects, presentations, performances, portfolios and field experience.

Direct Loan Program - Federal student loan program offering subsidized and unsubsidized Direct Stafford loans, federal Direct Consolidation loans, and Direct PLUS loans.

Discount Rate - The total institutional grant dollars as a percentage of gross tuition and fee revenue.

DSST - Exams designed to measure a student's competency in a specific subject matter; qualifying exam scores result in college credits awarded by participating institutions; program is offered through Prometric.

Dual Enrollment - A program offered at participating high schools that allows students to enroll in college-level courses; some credits will count toward both high school graduation requirements and a college degree.

Education Savings Accounts (ESA) - A qualified tuition program, typically set up by a state or eligible educational institution, which allows families to either prepay or contribute to an account established for paying a student's qualified educational expenses at an eligible educational institution.

Endowment - An institution's financial investments/portfolio designed to produce an income; a portion of the income is used to support an institution's annual priorities which may include scholarships.

Enrollment Status - A designation measured by the number of credits carried in a term; a student may be considered full-time, half-time, or less than half-time based on the number of credits attempted that term.

Expected Family Contribution (EFC) - A dollar figure the federal government has determined a family can contribute toward one year's college expenses; figure is based on information provided by a student and family when filing the FAFSA.

Expected Family Contribution (EFC) Calculators - An online tool used to give students and families an early estimate of their Expected Family Contribution (EFC).

Extended Repayment Plan - A federal loan repayment plan in which payments can be fixed or graduated; made for up to 25 years.

FAFSA4caster - An online tool that provides an estimate of federal financial aid for one academic year.

Federal Methodology - Formula used when reviewing a student's FAFSA to determine a student's Expected Family Contribution (EFC) and federal aid eligibility.

Federal Work-Study Program - Program that provides undergraduate and graduate students with part-time employment during the school year.

Fees - Typically a mandatory charge for a service or item not covered by tuition; could include, on the low end, a $5 ID or, on the high end, a $2,000 student health care plan.

Financial Aid - Funds from a number of sources to help meet a student and family's demonstrated financial need to cover educational expenses; sources for these funds include federal and state governments, colleges and universities, banks and other private lenders, as well as private and nonprofit organizations.

Financial Aid Administrator (FAA) - An institution's employee whose job is to coordinate a student's financial aid needs.

Financial Aid Shopping Sheet - A template for financial aid awards that clearly states the total cost of attendance, all grants and scholarships, net price, and the self-help options to pay the net price, including work-study and loans. More than 2,000 institutions have agreed to use this template.

Financial Fit - A college match that considers a student and family's ability to pay without incurring considerable debt.

Financial Need - The cost of attendance minus the Expected Family Contribution (EFC).

Forbearance - Period of time when a borrower can postpone making payments on a loan, typically due to financial hardships; interest continues to accrue during this time.

Free Application for Federal Student Aid (FAFSA) - The required financial aid form for all federal student aid and most institutional aid.

Full Pay - Refers to a student and family's ability to pay the full cost of attendance without financial aid.

Gap or Gapping - *See Unmet Need*

Gap Year - Alternative to college during the year immediately following a high school student's graduation; may be spent traveling, interning, working or other venture.

Gift Aid - Money that does not need to be paid back, primarily scholarships and grants.

Grace Period - Usually a specified number of months between a student's last semester of enrollment and when a first loan payment is due.

Graduated Repayment Plan - A federal loan repayment plan in which payments start out low and increase every two years; made for up to 10 years.

Graduation Rate - A measurement in percentages of students who start at a specific institution and graduate within a specific period of time from that institution.

Grant - Money provided to a student who typically shows financial need; this money is not repaid.

Income Based Repayment (IBR) Plan - A federal loan repayment plan in which payments are based on income and family size; designed primarily for lower income.

Income Contingent Repayment Plan - A federal loan repayment plan where payments are calculated each year and are based on income, family size, and the total amount owed on direct loans.

Income Sensitive Repayment Plan - A federal loan repayment plan where payments increase or decrease based on annual income.

Independent Students - Students who meet one or more of the following criteria: 24 years old, married, an orphan or ward of the court, a graduate or professional student, a veteran or active duty member of the U. S. Armed Forces, or economically responsible for legal dependents other than a spouse.

Institutional Grant - Money provided by a college or university to a student who typically shows financial need; this money is not repaid.

Institutional Methodology (IM) - Formula used by the College Board's need analysis system when reviewing a student's CSS/PROFILE; used to determine institutional aid eligibility.

Institutional Student Information Record (ISIR) - Version of a Student Aid Report (SAR) forwarded to a college or university.

Institutional Scholarship - Money provided by a college or university to a student typically for some type of merit, including academic or athletic, rather than financial need; this money is not repaid.

Interest Deduction - A federal tax deduction of up to $2,500 based on income and student loan payments.

International Baccalaureate (IB) - Rigorous courses/program offered to students at participating high schools; high scores on the IB exam may qualify students for college credits and/or placement in upper-level college courses; offered through the International Baccalaureate Organization.

Lender - A financial institution or entity, including the U.S. Department of Education, which provides loan funds to students and parents.

Lifetime Learning Credits - An IRS-approved tax credit of up to $2,000 based on income.

Loan Default Rate - A measurement in percentages of students from an institution who have defaulted on their student loans within the first two or three years.

Loan Forgiveness - The cancelation of a portion or remaining balance of a loan by a lender.

Loan Rehabilitation - The process borrowers would follow to re-qualify for federal financial aid if they had defaulted on a student loan.

Loan Servicer - A company that collects payments on a loan on behalf of a lender.

Massive Open Online Course (MOOC) - A free, online course, with no admission criteria, typically provided over 4-12 weeks, with assignments and evaluation of student work.

Merit-Based Aid - Money provided to a student typically for some type of ability or skill, including academic or athletic, rather than financial need; this money is not repaid.

Need Analysis - Formula used to determine a student's Expected Family Contribution (EFC) and aid eligibility.

Need-Aware - A process in which an admission decision takes into consideration a student and family's ability to pay the cost of attendance.

Need-Based Aid - Financial aid provided to a student based on financial need rather than merit.

Need-Blind - A process in which an admission decision does not take into consideration a student and family's ability to pay the cost of attendance.

Net Price - The cost of attendance minus all scholarships and grants; what a student and family will actually pay.

Net Price Calculator - An online tool used by institutions to provide an estimate of what a student and family will actually pay.

Parent Loans for Undergraduate Students (PLUS) - Loans for parents (Parent PLUS loans) or graduate students (Grad PLUS loans).

Pay As You Earn Repayment Plan - A federal loan repayment plan, designed for those with a partial financial hardship; based on income and family size; made over a period of 20 years.

Payment Plan - An option offered by an institution or company that spreads a student's bill payments out over a number of months.

Pell Grant - Federal money for undergraduate students with financial need; money is not repaid.

Perkins Loan - A federal loan made by an institution for students with exceptional financial need.

Personal Identification Number (PIN) - A requirement for students and parents when filing the FAFSA online; serves as an electronic signature.

Preferential Packaging - A financial aid and enrollment strategy used by institutions to attract the strongest students.

Prior Learning Assessment (PLA) - A measurement of knowledge obtained in a specific subject outside the classroom that can lead to awarding college credits; examples include CLEP, DSST and challenge exams.

Private Loans - Loans issued to borrowers by banks and other financial institutions; does not include federal loans.

Public Service Loan Forgiveness - Balance of a borrower's student loan is dismissed when certain requirements are met.

Qualified Tuition Programs (QTP) - *See 529 Plan*

Reach - Match - Safety - A college admission strategy used by students; typically chances for admission to a reach school are minimal, to a match school are likely, and to a safety school have a high probability.

Remedial Class - Instruction offered to students to better prepare them to handle college-level class.

Repayment Period - An agreed-upon period of time to repay a student loan.

Reverse Transfer - Relatively new trend allowing transfer students from a 2-year to a 4-year school to complete the required courses for an associate's degree simultaneously while working toward the bachelor's degree.

SAT - One of several standardized tests that may be taken by students planning to gain admission into college; offered by the College Board, a nonprofit organization.

Scholarship - Money provided to a student typically for some type of ability or skill, including academic or athletic, rather than financial need; this money is not repaid.

Self-Help Aid - Money that is earned or needs to be paid back; examples include work-study and loans.

Simplified Needs Test (SNT) - A designation for when specific income-driven requirements are met when filing the FAFSA; with an Adjusted Gross Income (AGI) below $50,000, all assets are excluded for federal aid consideration.

Stackable Certificates/Credentials - Short- and long-term education pathways that allow students to enter the workforce with a credential which can be built upon over time and lead to an associate's and/or a bachelor's degree.

Stafford Loan - A federal loan with two options: subsidized (government pays the interest while student is enrolled); or unsubsidized (interest accrues while student is enrolled in school.)

Standard Repayment Plan - A federal loan repayment plan with 120 equal monthly payments over a period of 10 years.

Sticker Price - The full cost of attendance for a term or academic year.

Student Aid Report (SAR) - A summary provided to a student who has filed a FAFSA; includes a student and family's Expected Family Contribution (EFC).

Subsidized Loan - A federal loan that requires the government to pay the interest while a student is enrolled in school.

Supplemental Educational Opportunity Grant (SEOG) - Federal money administered by an institution for undergraduate students with exceptional financial need; money is not repaid.

Teacher Loan Forgiveness - Balance of a borrower's student loan is dismissed when certain requirements are met.

TRIO Programs - Federally funded programs, typically targeting low-income, first-generation college students and adults, which help to prepare individuals to be college- and career-ready; programs include Educational Opportunity Centers, Student Support Services, Talent Search, and Upward Bound.

Tuition - A charge for instruction.

Tuition Discount Rate - Total institutional grant dollars as a percentage of gross tuition revenue.

Tuition Prepayment Program - A type of 529 plan which allows the payer to provide all or part of the amount of tuition for a student's college education.

Tuition Savings Accounts - A type of 529 plan which allows a donor to contribute to an account established for paying a student's qualified education expenses at an eligible educational institution.

Unmet Need - A gap created when the cost of attendance is not covered after subtracting all financial aid and the Expected Family Contribution (EFC).

Unsubsidized Loan - A federal loan that requires the interest to accrue while a student is enrolled in school.

Verification - A process that may occur when filing the FAFSA that requires additional documentation.

Index

About the Author

Mark Bilotta has been in the field of higher education for more than 25 years. He started in admissions, working at the College of the Holy Cross and Worcester State College. He served seven years on the President's Cabinet at Assumption College as Executive Assistant to the President where he oversaw public affairs as well as government and community relations. During that time, he also served as Secretary to the Board of Trustees.

In 2006, he was named CEO of the former Colleges of Worcester Consortium, an association of 13 public and private colleges that provided shared academic, administrative and student affair services for 35,000 students and 16,000 faculty and staff. At the same time, he oversaw a Massachusetts statewide network of TRIO and GEAR UP programs that serves more than 14,000 clients, mostly low-income, first-generation college goers. Mark currently serves as Chairman of the Board of that statewide network, now called Massachusetts Education and Career Opportunities, Inc. (MassEdCO).

A strong consumer advocate, Mark launched an independent complement to the College Scorecard called CollegeValue®. This free, online tool, found at collegevalue.info, measures the value and risk of enrolling at a specific college at a specific net price and has been compared to the Kelley Blue Book.

In addition to his writing and website work, Mark continues to speak with school counselors, parents and students about the need to choose colleges that are both a good academic and financial fit.

28748038R00060

Made in the USA
Charleston, SC
20 April 2014